slugs

just wanna have fun

by simon drew

An Introduction.

The slug is an animal both rare and secretive. Most people have never seen one but a lucky few have caught a glimpse as one disappears. Sometimes they are spotted at night in a car's headlights as they dart across a road.

The images in this book are the sum total of all known

slug encounters documented by science. Marvel at the array of slug behaviour (which is known in the USA as slug behavior). The drawings compiled here are a vital record of slugs in their natural habitat: because of environmental pressures and bird predation in some gardens their numbers have dwindled to a few million.

published by A.T.P. Gifts Ltd
Lower Wharf, Wallbridge,
Stroud, Glos. GL5 3JT
www.atpgifts.com

the slugman of alcatraz

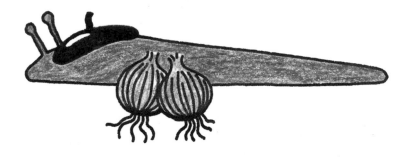

the french lieutenants slug

slugs of the caribbean

slow white and the 7 slugs

little red riding slug

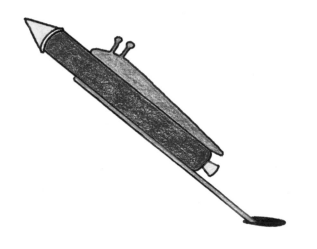

2001: a slug odyssey

one small step for a slug....

one flew over
the slugs nest

the little slug
on the prairie

gone with the slug

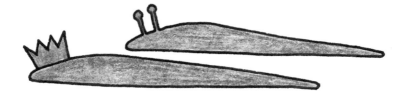

the slug and i

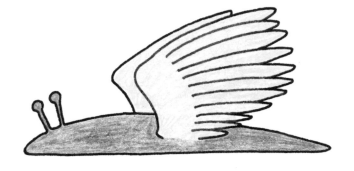

the slug has landed

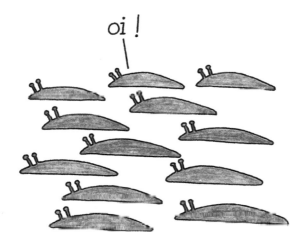

twelve angry slugs

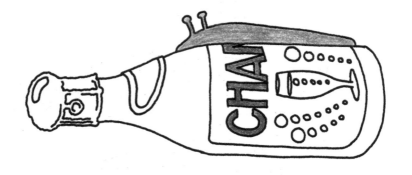

the slug that launched
a thousand ships

a slug is for life
not just for christmas

the slug of oz

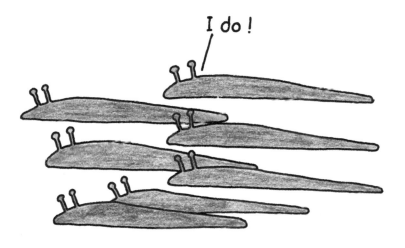

7 slugs for 7 brothers

wolfgang amadeus slug

stirling slug

a midsummer
night's slug

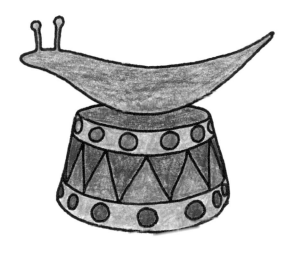

the taming of the slug

tinker, tailor, soldier, slug

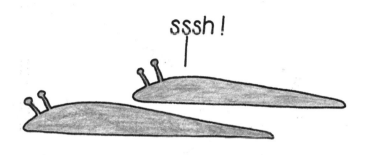

the silence of the slugs

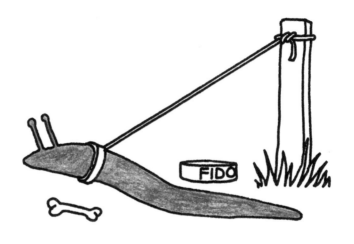

slug of the baskervilles

slug trek

horatio slug

slug of notre dame

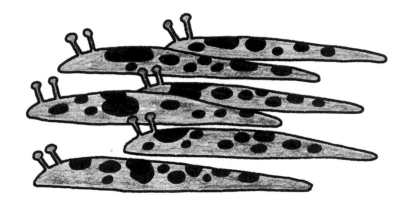

101 slugs

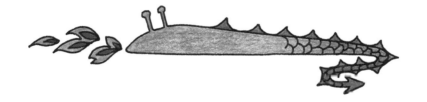

puff the magic slug

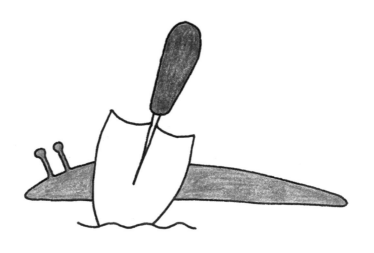

capability slug

chelsea flower slug

lady jane slug

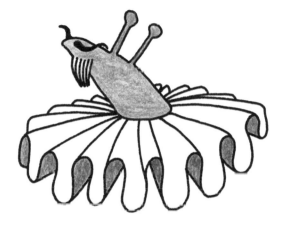

the laughing slug

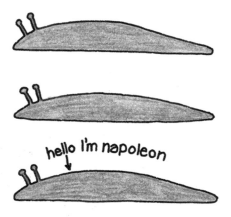

the madness
of slug the third

dance of the 7 slugs

the seven deadly slugs

hannibal first tried
to cross the alps
with slugs

SLUG

on
board

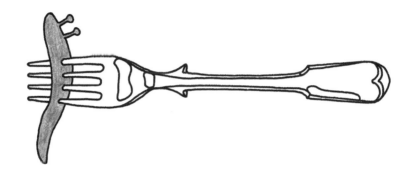

never eat a slug unless
there's an 'r' in the month

red slug at night
shepherd's delight

one slug doesn't
make a summer

slug of liberty

superslug

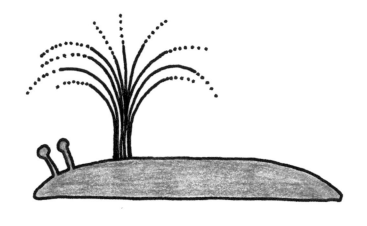

moby slug

slug of whisky

slugsy malone

captain corelli's slug

stand by your slug

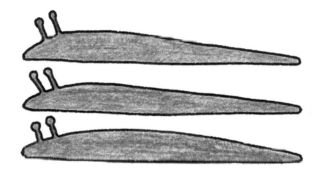

vera, chuck and dave

a game of slugs
and ladders

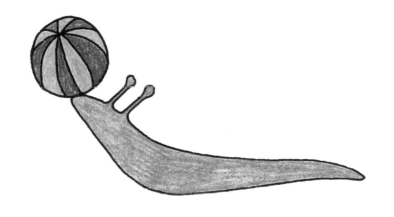

you can't teach
an old slug new tricks

'lettuce pray'

slug of arc

let sleeping slugs lie

the darling slugs
of may

beware of slugs
bearing gifts

slug von trapp
(with lonely goat)

to kill a mocking slug

sluggage

ask not what a slug can
do for you; ask what you
can do for a slug.